COPYRIGHT

BANKING FOR TEENS AND STUDENTS BOOK & STUDY GUIDE

No part of this book or eBook should be reproduced, transmitted, downloaded, decompiled, reverse engineered, or restored in or introduced into any information storage and retrieval system, in any form, or by any means. Whether it is electronic or mechanical, now know or hereinafter invented without the expressed written of the copyright owner.

This is a work of real life places and incidents, which are used to inspire, encourage, and help others through different areas of transitioning with Banking. These are experiences through the authors' real life.

The reverse engineering and uploading of Books or eBooks via internet or any other means without permission of the copyright owner is illegal and punishable by law.

Please purchase Paperback or eBook only authorized.

Your support of the author`s rights are appreciated.

Book

Banking for Teens and Students Books & Study Guide VOLUME 6

ISBN-10: 1535011394

ISBN-13: 978-1535011396

Author: Bridget C. Williams

Publisher: CreateSpace Independent Publishing Platform (June 29, 2016)

Copyright©2016 Bridget C. Williams

All rights reserved.

BANKING FOR TEENS AND STUDENTS BOOKS & STUDY GUIDE

Author Bridget C. Williams

CONTENT

Banks and Credit Unions	2
Checking Account	5
Balancing a Check Book	14
Savings Account	17
Banking Fees	19
Bank Deposits	27
ATM Machines	33
Bank Statements	39
Online Banking	44
Telephone and Mobile Banking	48
Credit Cards	51
Credit Card Safety	57

BANKS OR CREDIT UNIONS

What is a Bank?

An establishment authorized by a government to accept deposits, pay interest, clear checks make loans, act as an intermediary in financial transactions, and provide other financial services to its customers.

What is a Credit Union?

Credit unions are owned and controlled by the people, or members, who use their services. Credit unions offer numerous financial products that help people maximize their incomes and increase their savings, often with fewer or lower fees than traditional banks. ... Credit union members, like bank customers, have access to checking and savings accounts, CDs, loan products.

Credit Union

Some schools offer this service called the in-school branch.

Banks and Credit Unions both

Yours savings account becomes another person or member's loan.

What's the **difference between** bank and credit union?

Bank

Credit Union

What is the **same between** a Bank and Credit Union?

Bank

Credit Union

BANK ACCOUNTS

CHECKING ACCOUNT

Basics

The primary benefit of getting a checking account is the ability to write checks.

Checks can be used:

- ☐ To pay bills at a store
- ☐ Give a person a check if you are short of cash, and will have the money in your account before they cash it.
- ☐ Send a check through the mail or electronically.
- ☐ Checks allow you to pay for things without having to carry large amounts of cash.
- ☐ **Very important to know** - writing a check or receiving a check does not guarantee the money is in the bank, unlike an ATM.

If you are going to use a check at a store you will be asked to provide specific information.

- ☐ Your address
- ☐ Phone number
- ☐ Show a photo ID
- ☐ Your driver's license number
- ☐ Other

Most banks are allowing their checking account customers to pay online. Which is better for you because you actually get to see if you have enough money or not. When you do your payments online you get a confirmation number after the transaction.

This is beneficial to the store or person receiving a check directly from the bank is because--before the bank issues "your" check, it makes sure you have the money in the account and deducts it immediately from your available funds (money).

Most vendors (stores) will not accepts checks because when they go to cash the check it bounces, because of the lack of funds. If your check bounces they may post your picture in the store or have you on a list. This could be really embarrassing for you. So, don't do it.

When you open an account, one of the first things you will do is to order your checks. **However, it's up to you**. Frequently the bank will pay for your first set of basic checks or charge you just a minimum fee.

Process of checks

- ☐ Ordering checks for a fee
- ☐ Checks come in different colors or an interesting design.
- ☐ There are also different styles of check books, so see which one works best for you.

All checks will have your name on them, your address, and telephone number. They are given number sequence on the right hand top corner.

Most people don't put the telephone number (although perhaps you might want to withhold it on a printed check for security reasons), along with another form of identification (photo ID is preferred).

When your checks arrive be sure to confirm that all the printed material is correct. There will also be a separate book (depending on the style of checks you ordered) called the **Check Transaction Register**. This has an area so you can record the information about each check, shows deposits, withdrawals, fees, and balances. Whatever you do, you always need to know how much money is in your account so you don't write a check for more than you have (**this is called bouncing a check**).

Bouncing a Check

If you bounce a check, the person you made it out to will be very mad. Second, your bank will probably charge you a hefty fee, probably $25 or more, for the bounced check. The bank may or may not cover your account for the overdrawn amount until you make a deposit to cover the outstanding amount.

Over Draft Protection

Some banks automatically enroll you in an over-draft protection plan. You might write a check for $20, it bounced and you then owe the bank not only the $20 but an additional $25 fee for the bounced check, and overdraft if you have the over draft.

This is the smart thing to do.

Some people will make a deposit and then write a check. If your deposit doesn't clear by the time the bank get your check, you are overdrawn. **Check with**

your bank to make sure your deposit has cleared before you write a check. Sometimes a check can take 5-7 business days to clear.

This is a sample filled check

YOUR NAME HERE		6244
YOUR ADDRESS	**SAMPLE FILLED**	
CITY, PROVINCE, POSTAL CODE	**CHEQUE**	DATE 2 0 1 6 1 0 3 0
000-000-000		Y Y Y Y M M D D

PAY TO THE ORDER OF ___JANE DOE (Who do you want to pay)___ $ 100.52

___One Hundred Dollars-------------------------------------52___ /100 DOLLARS 🔒 Security features included. Details on back.

YOUR FINACIAL INSTITUTION
YOUR ADDRESS
CITY, PROVINCE, POSTAL CODE
000-000-000

MEMO ___Paid for Tutoring- Jane Doe___   ___You sign here___   NP

⑈6244⑈ ⑆12345⑇678⑈ 123⑈456⑈78

Adjusting your Life Style
Frugal Spending B. Williams

Do not accept any checks unless they are from a well known bank or credit union.

NOW IT'S YOUR TURN TO FILL IN THE CHECK

```
_____                                              6244
_____        FILL IN THE
_____        BLANK CHECK
_____                          DATE  2 0  __  __
                                             Y Y Y Y  M M  D D

PAY TO THE
ORDER OF _____  $_____

_____/100 DOLLARS

_____
_____
_____
_____
MEMO _____              MP

⑆6244⑆  ⑈12345⑈678⑇  123⑆456⑆78
```

- **Check Number:** The number of your check (upper right hand corner, also one of the numbers on the bottom of the check). It is a good idea when you pay a bill to write the check number, date, and amount you paid on the invoice (bill) for your records.

- **Date:** Put in the correct date. Month/day/year. Banks won't take a check dated in the future. Which is called post-dated check.

- **Pay to the Order Of (or Payable to):** Make sure to complete and use the correct name of the person or company to whom you are writing the check. No nicknames! If you call your friend Betty, but his legal name is Roberta and that is what is on her checking account, you need to write Roberta and her last name also.

- **Dollar sign $ Numerical:** Put the dollar amount of the check in numbers. Start writing the numbers close to the printed dollar sign. It has to be legible. Put in the decimal point for cents ($60.44). If you leave too much room, $ 60.44, a dishonest person might add a digit before the first digit 6… like $160.44).

- **Dollars (amount written in words):** This is where you write the amount of the check in words for the whole dollars (Sixty dollars), and a fractional figure (44/100) for amounts less than a dollar. This is how that bank confirms the amount in case your hand writing is not legible. Also, draw a straight line to fill up the remaining space on the line ending with the word "Dollars", like this:

- Sixty Dollars --------------- 44/100.

- **Signature Line:** The line on the far right is for your signature. Use the correct name you used when you opened your account. As you get older your signature may change. You also fill out a signature card which your bank keeps in case there's a question about your signature. When you go a different branch, the bank may ask your own branch to send a copy of your signature card to make sure you are who you say you are and the signature matches.

- **Memo:** Usually a space on the bottom left, opposite the signature line. Use this line to put your account number if you are paying a bill, or any other information that may help the person processing your payment to identify your account, service provide and the person's name will help you keep track of your payments as well.

- **Numbering at the Bottom:** This is like a bar code on merchandise, it lets banks and credit unions know how to handle the transaction. There are three groups of numbers at the bottom of each check separate with a: (need symbol at bottom of check bold vertical dash with bold squared colon). Some banks put these numbers in different order. My bank puts the TRANSIT number first, the account number second and the check number third (some banks put the check number between the routing and account number):

- **Bank Transit Number:** This is a three to nine digit number that banks in **YOUR COUNTRY** use to identify the financial institution (bank) on which the check is drawn.

BALANCING A CHECK BOOK

Balancing Your Check Book

Each month you will receive a bank statement by mail unless you have agreed to receive it online. Carefully look over your statement. Place a checkmark in your transaction book next to all the items that are also on your statement. Take note if there are any differences. Add any interest the bank has paid you; subtract any fees the bank may have charged (make sure they are legitimate). Subtract any checks that might not have cleared. If you find any discrepancies between your numbers and the bank's you have a little detective work to do. You need to find out why. This is not fun, but necessary.

Using a transaction registry... most bank books have this in the back.

Transaction Registry

THIS IS GENERALLY AT THE BACK OF THE BANK BOOK A FORM OF FINANCIAL RECORD KEEPING.

Start by checking your math; make sure all your additions and subtractions are correct. Subtract the balance in your transaction register from the balance statement. Does the amount match the amount of one of your transactions? If you still find an error, or see an inappropriate fee, contact your bank.

It is a good idea to create a cushion at the bank. Keep a little extra in your account, a certain minimum balance, in case of an emergency or you forget to record a transaction. You never want to bounce a check or have your bank call you saying you have insufficient funds. This can cost you dearly, with additional fees/penalty or loss of interest, if that applies.

Periodically review the type of bank account(s) you have.

Have your circumstances changed?

Is this still the correct type of account for you need?

SAVINGS ACCOUNT

- You open a savings account at the bank or credit union.
- The bank pays you interest on the money that you deposit and leave in that account.
- The bank and credit union then loans that money out to other people, only they charge a slightly higher interest rate on the loan than what they pay you for your account.

The difference in interest they pay you verses the interest they charge others is part of how they stay in business.

Interest on savings accounts is usually compounded daily and paid each month. About **compounded interest** the bank is paying you interest on the money you have in your account. That means that if your account earns one percent interest, then each day 1/365th of that one percent of the amount of money you have in your savings account is then added to your total. Here is the calculation:

It's very important that you ask what interested is on your bank account so that you are aware of it. The amount of interest your money earns in a savings account often depends on the bank or credit union you have selected and the type of account as well.

The basic savings account gives you a bank book or pass book (*for the savings account- it's similar to the transaction registry*). This account will usually have either no minimum balance requirement or a low one, but will offer a very low interest rate (*meaning your money won't earn that much*).

Some accounts banks offer for Teens and Students based on the bank and the Country you live in.

- TFSA Account -Tax Free Savings Account
- No limit accounts
- Student Account
- Youth Savings Account
- And other accounts which they will gladly explain to you.

See if you can find an account that doesn't charge a fee. Do the research with your parents if they have to sign for you.

All banks have products remember think frugal to save money.

BANKS AND CREDIT UNIONS DO CHARGE A FEE.

Costs Involved

Sometimes, but not always, banks charge fees for having a savings account. The fee may be low -- like a dollar a month -- or it may be higher or it could even be based on your balance. For this reason, you should always shop around and compare what different banks are offering. Things you should look at include:

Fees and services charges on the account

Minimum balance requirements (Some banks charge a fee only if you don't keep a certain amount of money in your account at all times.) It is also based on the account type.

Interest rate paid on your balance

What happens once you have a savings account?

When you open a savings account you'll get a small book called a register (like a check book register) where you write your beginning balance (the amount you originally deposit) and all of your future deposits and withdrawals. This tool helps you keep track of how much money you have.

The statement will list all of your transactions as well as any fees charged to your account and interest your money has earned. In order to make sure you didn't forget to write down any withdrawals and/or deposits (and also to double-check the bank's activities) you should go through each entry in your register and compare it with the bank's statement. They should match up -- this is referred to as reconciling your account. If they don't, you'll need to find your mistake and correct it in your register (unless it is a bank error, but that isn't very common).

The only other thing is to remember to make deposits into your account and sit back and watch your money grow!

QUESTION YOU NEED TO ASK FOR CHECKING AND SAVINGS ACCOUNT – Actually go to the bank and ask the below questions with you parents. You can actually call and set up an appointment with the bank based on your parents' approval.

What are the banks hours, and where can I actually go into the bank and speak to someone if I need to?

what are the age limits for the different accounts that would benefit you? Let the bank or credit union know that you may be interested in opening an account (checking vs. saving)?

Do my parent(s) have to be co-signature(s) on my account?

What is the minimum amount I have to put in to open an account?

Is there a minimum amount I have to keep in the account so that I won't be charged a monthly fee?

Will I be penalized if I don't keep my money in the account for a certain amount of time?

What, if any, are the monthly service fees?

What services does the bank offer?

[   ]

Does the bank charge for these services and how much? Determine what service you might need and compare the rates.

[   ]

DON'T EVER DO THIS

Beware of making a check out to cash. Anyone can cash this check. If someone steals your purse/wallet and finds a check made out to cash, they can just go to their bank and redeem it. It is a much better practice to write out the person's name or business. If you want money, write a check out to yourself.

SOME OTHER QUESTIONS YOU CAN ASK THE BANK

Does the bank provide free fee accounts?

What are the fees for?

- ✓ Money Orders
- ✓ Cashier's Check (also known as bank check, official check, demand draft, teller's check, bank draft or treasure's check - which is a check guaranteed by the bank)
- ✓ Traveler's Checks

The bank will gladly explain the Difference of each product

What is a money order? It's a printed order for payment of a specified sum of money, issued by a bank, credit union, or post office. Also ask about the fee for money orders.

What did the bank or credit union tell you?

What is a cashier check? Cashier's checks are checks issued by banks, and they're used when somebody wants to be sure that they'll really get paid. If you're paying with a cashier's check, funds move out of your account immediately when you request the check. You can walk into any bank or credit union.

What did the bank or credit union tell you?

What is a Travellers check? Travellers Check is a convenient and safe way to carry funds for travel. They are accepted worldwide but unlike cash, which is gone for good in the event of theft or loss, they can be replaced or refunded, usually within 24 hours anywhere in the world.

What did the bank or credit union tell you?

BANK DEPOSITS

How to Make A Deposit

Deposits are a good thing. That is when you are putting money into the bank. You can put either cash or checks into the bank. Either way, you must fill out a deposit slip, (not if you go to the teller, or the ATM machine).

If you deposit a check (assuming it is made out to you), and you want to deposit it, turn the check over and you will see an "Endorse Here" section. Sign your name. On the next line put the words "For Deposit Only", and then on the third line put your account number.

When you first receive your checks you will also receive either separate deposit slips, or it will be included at the back of your check book. Generic Deposit slips are also available at your bank and at the bank's ATM machine. At the ATM machine envelopes are provided to make your deposit (include your endorsed checks and a deposit slip). If you don't have your slip and are using the bank's generic deposit slip you must fill in your account number and name.

What Question would you like to ask about Your Deposits ?

1.

2.

3.

4.

5.

6.

7.

8.

DEPOSIT SLIPS MAY VARY BASED ON THE FINANCIAL INSTITUTION TTHIS IS A SAMPLE COPY

PRE-FILLED DEPOSIT SLIP

Adjusting your Life Style
Frugal Spending -B. Williams

Name
Full Address

DATE January 4, 2015

Your signature
SIGN HERE FOR CASH RECEIVED (IF REQUIRED)
DEPOSITS MAY NOT BE AVAILABLE FOR IMMEDIATE WITHDRAWAL

Bank Name
Bank Full Address

CHECKS 3021

CHECK OR TOTAL FROM OTHER SIDE
SUB-TOTAL
LESS CASH RECEIVED

$4 0 0
$32 5 0

$36 5 0

$ 36.50

⑆012345678⑆ 01234567890123⑈

Bank Routing Number   **Bank Account Number**

Make sure your bank account is provided, add it to the slip for your security. Include the Routing/Transit Number as well ---if it is not on the slip.

Banking for Teens and Students- Book and Study Guide ---Adjusting Your Life Style by Bridget C. Williams

NOW IT'S YOUR TURN TO FILL OUT THE DEPOSIT SLIP

- **Date:** First line on the left. Note: deposits may not be available for immediate withdrawal. Banks need to clear checks first, unless you presently have sufficient funds to cover that amount.

- **Sign Here for Cash Received if Required:** If you would like cash back (under date line).

- **Cash:** The first line on the upper right would be the total amount of "Cash", if you're depositing coins or dollar bills.

- **Checks:** The second line down on the right and on the back would be for your checks. On the line to the left put in the check number. Then put in the dollar and cents amount. If you have hit the jackpot and need more room to enter checks, use the back.

- **Subtotal:** Line for the total amount of checks and cash you are depositing.

- **Less Cash Received:** Put in the amount you want to withdraw, if any.

- **$:** This is the bottom line with the dollar sign for the total amount you are depositing. In most cases, since you'll be making deposits separately from withdrawing cash, this will be the same as your subtotal line.

Now it`s time to fill in the Bank Deposit Form on the next page.

FILL IN THE DEPOSIT SLIP

DATE _____
DEPOSITS MAY NOT BE AVAILABLE FOR IMMEDIATE WITHDRAWAL

_____
SIGN HERE FOR CASH RECEIVED (IF REQUIRED)

Checks

CHECK OR TOTAL FROM OTHER SIDE ▶

Sub-total ▶

LESS CASH RECEIVED ▶

TOTAL $

Bank Routing Number   **Bank Account Number**

Adjusting your Life Style
Frugal Spending - B. Williams

ATM MACHINES

ATM - Automatic Teller Machine Card

When you have a checking account (sometimes even special high yield saving accounts) you might qualify for an Automatic Teller Machine Card (ATM), which allows you to withdraw cash from a machine. Most ATM machines at a bank will also allow you to deposit money, transfer money and check your account balance.

These ATM cards are debit cards.
Before an ATM machine dispenses (gives) cash, it checks to see if you have adequate funds (money) available for that amount. If not you won't be able to make a withdrawal. Your bank will also limit the amount of cash you can withdraw on a given day, which may be as small as $20 or it could be as large as $100 (or more), regardless of how much you have in your account.

It really depend on how long you been with the bank and had your accounts. This will be based on the type of account you have and the amount of money you keep in the bank. Check with your bank for approval. The amount you can withdraw can be negotiated.

Note: all ATM machines are not programmed the same way. Some ATM machines might have different amounts of money you are permitted to withdraw.

Here is a sample ATM RECIEPT. Just keep saving your pennies and your account can look like this.

```
            SAMPLE  ATM RECIEPT
                      ⚘
               Adjusting your Life Style
               Frugal Spending -B. Williams

TERMINAL #            =     D201[
SEQUENCE #            =     19212
AUTH     #            =     03241 00
DATE            02/05/2004  22:54:28

CARD NUMBER                 XXXXXXXXXXX)

CUSTOMER NAME                  DOE

DISPENSED AMOUNT      =       $60.00
REQUESTED AMOUNT      =       $60.00
FROM ACCOUNT                 checking
TERMINAL FEE          =        $1.25

TOTAL AMOUNT          =       $61.25
BALANCE               =    $629,112.23
```

When the bank issues you an ATM card they will also issue you a PIN number, Personal Identification

Number (for security). Most banks will allow you to change your pin number to one that you find easy to remember. **This is crucial** -Never give your PIN number to anyone else! When you go to an ATM machine you will need to insert your ATM Card and type in your Pin Number.

If you enter the wrong number more than two or three times the machine will shut down and you will not be able to make any transactions. **If this happens make sure you contact your bank at once.** The machine might also capture your card. Although machines are different, most only allow you to make withdrawals in $20 denominations (some occasionally $10). **Be careful of ATM fees! If you use a different institution or just a local ATM the fees are much higher.**

Debit Card: **Combined ATM & Debit Card**

Although you can get one or both of the above type debit cards, this combo card, often just referred to as the "Debit Card" is the most popular. It can function both as an ATM card. Most Debit Cards are associated with the major credit cards of VISA or MasterCard. You can use them wherever these cards are accepted, such as stores, gas stations, restaurants etc.

You will receive a PIN number with these cards. **Do not use tap** on your card if it's get stolen or lost you could lose lots of money. Sometimes you can just present the card and sign with your pin number. This method is much safer to use. One of the benefits is - that some stores will allow you to get additional cash above the amount of your purchase. Say you spend $100 at a supermarket—you can get an extra $20 back in cash, making your total purchase $120. You should only do this if you have the money in your account and it is for a need not a want.

Remember, you can only use a Debit Card if you have sufficient money in your account to cover your purchase. When you are using a regular credit card it is like issuing an IOU. It creates a loan obligation to the Credit Card Company and sometimes huge interest charges. ***This will be discussed in the credit card section.***

For young users, even most adults, a Debit Card is the best way to go. If you don't have the money in the bank, you won't be able to spend it, and you won't go into debit or have a credit problem!

Additional Basics and clarification

If you have a checking account with a bank, you are offered different ways to access your money other than using a check or a credit card. You may qualify to receive a plastic card, which can be an ATM (Automatic Teller Machine) Card, Debit Card, or a card with combined features. When you want to get cash or make a purchase, you put your card in a machine, enter a pin number (**a secret identification number**), type in the amount you want to withdraw or use to pay a bill (**not necessarily in this order**) and the machine will check to see if you have the money in the bank. If you do, the transaction will be processed and you can receive your cash. If you don't, it will deny the transaction.

This is one way to make sure you don't spend more than you have in the bank. If you use your card other than in a branch of your bank, there might be additional fees for the use of the ATM. You will always be shown what the fee is. You can agree to accept the fee and proceed with your transaction or, deny it and you get your card back and your transaction will not be processed. If it does go into the bank right away or call them and keep your transaction slip.

You can pay your bills at the ATM machine, online, telephone banking, or teller service. You have so many options.

Does your Bank provide fees for these some of these additional services, some bank do based on your account?

PROVIDE	FEES – Yes or No
Money Orders	
Cashier Checks	
Bank Drafts	
Travelers Check	

This would depend on the type of bank account you have.

Does the bank provide free Notary Services (proof of signature on legal documents)?

FIND OUT WHAT OTHER SERVICES THE BANK OFFERS, THAT COULD BE BENEFICIAL

BANK STATEMENTS

A bank statement is a record typically sent to the account holder every month which shows all transaction on your account.

BREAKING DOWN 'Bank Statement'

During reconciliation of their account with the bank's records, account holders should check their statement for discrepancies(mistakes). Account holders must report discrepancies in writing as soon as possible. A bank statement is also referred to as an account statement. It shows the money you have left over in your account, deposits, and removal of funds.

A bank issues a bank statement to an account holder that shows the detailed activity in the account. It allows the account holder to see all the transactions processed on his account. Banks usually send monthly statements to an account holder on a set date by mail or email. In addition, transactions on a statement typically appear in chronological order. The last transaction will be the most recent transaction on the statement.

The bank statement lists checks paid, total withdrawals, total deposits, interest earned and service charges or penalties incurred on an account. In addition, it provides the beginning balance, ending balance, statement date, transaction date for each transaction, payee, customer name and address, statement period, the account holder's account number and the bank's customer service number.

Sample Bank Statement
Your Name

Type of Account   **Date**

Date	Transactions	Payment	Deposit	Balance
April 1	Balance b/f			800.50 Cr
April 3	Cash deposit		7,000.00	7,800.50 Cr
April 4	Transfer from branch		2,500.00	10,300.50 Cr
April 6	Cheque book	5.00		10,295.50 Cr
April 8	70010 *(Check Numbers)*	550.00		9,745.50 Cr
April 10	70011	700.00		9,045.50 Cr
April 12	70012	430.00		8,615.50 Cr
April 15	Bank GIRO Credit		645.00	9,260.50 Cr
April 20	Direct Debit	574.00		8,686.50 Cr
April 25	Interest		166.70	8,853.20 Cr
April 28	Bank Charges	10.00		8,843.20 Cr

THE STATEMENT WILL SHOW YOU THESE ITEMS ON THE NEXT PAGE.

Check Number: The number is shown on the upper right hand side of the check (also on the bottom). Checks are in order. If you make an error on a check, still write the check number and then write "Void" across the check and record it in your registry. This way it won't show you missing a check.

Date: The day you write on the check. **Note:** Just because you write the check, the person/merchant receiving the check might not immediately bring it to their bank to deposit. Furthermore, banks often take a few days to process your check. If you write a check on March 15st, and you receive your statement on April 1st, there is a chance it won't be included in that statement.

Description of Transaction: Record who the check was made out to. Not only do you need to include all payments made, but also all withdrawals (and for your records what it might have been used for). If you use an ATM or purchase something with a debit card you need to include that amount as well. If you use a debit card, and incur a fee for your usage, you need to indicate that also. If you pay online, the bank will give you a confirmation number code, you might wish to include this also, along with the payee information. You need to keep one source for all your transactions in order to reconcile your bank statements (make sure they are correct).

Payment Amount: The amount you wrote the check for.

Withdrawal Amount: The amount of money you took out.

Fee Amount: Any fees that might be incurred during a transaction. The main fees will be from ATM machines that are not associated with your bank. Also based on the type of account you have the bank may impose a monthly service fee which also must be deducted.

Deposit Amount: Money you put into the account.

Transfer: If you have more than one account and move money from a checking to a savings account or one account to another.

Balance: Based on the kind of transaction you made, add or subtract that amount from the previous balance to come up with your new current balance. Let's say you had $200 in the bank, you wrote a check for $50 to purchase new clothes at a store, and your new balance is now $150). Make sure you correctly add (if you put money into your account), or subtract (if you take money out or put it into another account).

CREATE YOUR OWN BANK STATEMENT

Date	Description	Withdrawals	Deposits	Balance

ONLINE BANKING

Online banking, also known as **internet banking**, **e-banking** or **virtual banking**, is an electronic payment system that enables customers of a **bank** or other financial institution to conduct a range of financial transactions through the financial institution's website.

Punch in your bank Webpage Account

For security notice on the left hand side you will see a green lock which means it secure to proceed with your transactions. However, if it is normally green in color. If this is not green do not proceed for your security.

This page will show: Punch in this information.

Client card number requested:

_____

Your password requested:

_____

Click the sign or login in button

There is a button that says **remember me**. Don`t do it your personal login information will be easy for anyone using your computer to obtain your personal banking information.

Another security measure is to Setup Question verifications so that you are not compromised. They have a list of questions, and you can add your own questions also. Once this is set up the questions will pop every time you log in and is a safety precaution.

Than you press continue

Depending on the bank you are using and what you have attached to your Bank Card.

You can do bill payments, Visa payments, Line of Credit Payments. Open new bank accounts, apply for other financial products.

You can see your Banking information:
- ✓ Bank accounts
- ✓ Credit cards
- ✓ Line of credit
- ✓ Visa card

Click the account you want to use.

Your information and transactions will show up an online bank statement pops up of current transactions.

Date	Description	Withdrawals	Deposits	Balance

You can also print of your bank statement. You can have them emailed it to you each month and you can print also.

This give you lots of options there are other things you can apply for but don`t unless you have your parents' consent.

You can do pre-authorized payment that come out each month which you don`t have to worry about this like rent, bill`s, donations.

TELEPHONE BANKING & MOBILE BANKING

Telephone banking is a service provided by a bank or other financial institution that enables customers to perform a range of financial transactions over the telephone, without the need to visit a bank branch or automated teller machine.

Mobile banking is a service provided by a bank or other financial institution that allows its customers to conduct a range of financial transactions remotely using a mobile device such as a mobile phone or tablet, and using software, usually called an app, provided by the financial institution for the purpose.

Call the telephone number on the back of your Bank Card to speak to someone or do your bill transactions or transferring money transaction. You can do the transactions yourself or you can speak to a customer representative to help you.

You will be asked to provide specific information only you will know regarding your banking information. This is for your security.

They will check your bank account balance, transactions; you can also have them do the bill payment for you by telephone. This is great when you are out of town and don't have computer access.

Customer Service will assist you with banking problems or concerns they will try their best to assist you. Customer Service may try to provide products that may benefit your circumstances or put you through to the appropriate department.

If you have questions regarding your visa, or loans, bank account, they will gladly assist you or can forward you to the department which specializes in that area.

Mobile Banking gives you an option to check your bank accounts similar features to online banking and telephone banking. However you must install banking application from your financial institution to activate this feature. The bank will show you how to set this up.

CREDIT CARDS

Credit card is the banks money which they loan you. **Some very important things you need to know about Credit cards that they don't tell you.** When you get your first credit card, usually in your late teens, it's a sort of fork in the road of your financial life.

One path leads to a lifetime of playing catch-up with ever-increasing debt, the other to lower interest rates, rewards, and easier to obtain loans. **Every scent you use on a credit card must be paid back with interest.**

Would you loan/give money to someone you didn't know? Or to someone you know has repeatedly failed to pay back money they borrowed? Not if you're smart.

Please answer the above question? Why or Why not?

Credit card companies are very smart. Cards issued to people new to the credit game. Typically come with higher than average interest rates and worse than average rewards (if any). This is because in their eyes you are an unknown quantity.

Only get a credit card if you are going to be smart about it. When you use it, pay it off each time. You don't want to end up 20 years later paying off the card. This is what can happen if you are not responsible with a credit card. If you don't have a job to pay this bill than don't get it.

This is something you don't want to do is have more than one credit card. The interest rates alone will consume you.

Juggling multiple credit card accounts at once can be tricky, so you want to avoid having more cards than you can keep track of. One smart method is to have one card for your specific purposes, and setting them to be automatically paid off in full each month. If you have more than one credit card…. That is lots of interest you will end up paying on top of the outstanding amount.

For instance

Bank Credit card 11% - 29% or higher

Store Credit Card - 20%- 29% or higher

If it is mandatory go with the lowest rate credit card. Don't look for perks because the interest rate will be much higher.

How many credit cards are in your wallet?

CREATE YOUR CARD LIST

CREDIT CARD	INTEREST	OUTSTANDING AMT.	TOTAL

WHY IS IT SO IMPORTANT TO YOU?

WHAT IS WRONG WITH HAVING ONE CARD? WHY OR WHY NOT?

DO YOU HAVE A PLAN? WHY OR WHY NOT?

WHAT ARE THE BENEFITS OF THIS?

ARE YOU KEEPING A LOW LIMIT? WHY OR WHY NOT?

ARE YOU STAYING ON TRACK? ARE YOU GETTING HELP?

DO YOU PAY IN FULL OR A PORTION?

HOW MANY CARDS DO YOU HAVE?

HAVE YOU LOOKED AT TERMS AND CONDITIONS? WHY AND WHY NOT?

HOW DOES IT MAKE YOU FEEL?

CREDIT CARD SAFETY

This is crucial part of your protection against fraud and identity theft.

- ✓ **Sign your card**

Sign the back of your credit card as soon as you receive it as a way to protect yourself if your card is ever stolen.

HAVE YOU EVER BEEN A VICTIM OF FRAUD? WHAT WAS STOLEN?

```
┌─────────────────────────────────────────┐
│                                         │
│                                         │
└─────────────────────────────────────────┘
```

- ✓ **Protect your personal identification number (PIN)**

Many credit cards require you to enter your PIN before you use them. Don't let anyone else see your PIN when you enter it into a card reader or ATM. Choose a number you can remember and don't carry any record of it in your wallet.

HOW OFTEN DO YOU CHANGE YOU PIN NUMBER?

- ✓ **Protect your card information when you shop by phone**

Never give out your credit card number unless you initiated the call and you know that you are dealing with a legitimate business. Also never give your card number out over a cordless phone. Radio scanners that eavesdrop on these conversations are available for a few hundred dollars at any electronics store.

HAVE YOU EXPERIENCED THIS? OR ACTUALLY DONE IT AND WHY?

- ✓ **Keep track of your card when you use it**

If you can, watch when the sales person processes your purchase. Make sure they don't take an extra copy of your card. Also be sure to get your card back after you use it.

HAVE YOU EVER FORGOTTEN YOUR CARD AFTER MAKING A PURCHASE?

```
┌─────────────────────────────────────────────┐
│                                             │
│                                             │
│                                             │
└─────────────────────────────────────────────┘
```

✓ Check your monthly statement

Make sure all the charges on your statement are yours. If you find something wrong, notify the card issuer right away.

HOW OFTEN DO YOU DO THIS? WHY OR WHY NOT?

```
┌─────────────────────────────────────────────┐
│                                             │
│                                             │
│                                             │
└─────────────────────────────────────────────┘
```

✓ Shred credit card statements and receipts

Destroy any voided or cancelled sales slips yourself. And cut up expired credit cards.

ARE YOU WILLING TO TRY THIS?

- ✓ **Keep a list** of all your cards

PUT EACH CARD IN THIS SPACE

- ✓ **Make a list of card numbers**

Expiration dates, and the toll-free numbers of your credit card companies. Keep this record in a safe place, separate from where you keep your cards. Use this information if you ever have to report your cards lost or stolen.

Your car List

1.
2.
3.
4.

✓ Carry only the cards you need

Especially when traveling. To clarify: you may need 1 card. You will not need 6.

FOLLOW THESE INSTRUCTION

✓ Never lend your card to anyone

Don't leave cards or receipts lying around your room, no matter where you live.

HAVE YOU EVER DONE THIS? WHY?

- ✓ **Credit card over the telephone**

Don't give your account number over the phone unless you've initiated the call. If you've dialed a wrong number, don't give it out at all.

HAVE YOU EVER DONE THIS?

- ✓ **Security**

Get a card that has added security features, like a photo ID. You will be a lot safer.

ARE YOU WILLING TO TRY THIS?

SMART TIPS

Send your creditors a change of address when you move.

- ☑ Take steps to protect your cards.
- ☑ Don't give your credit card or checking account number to anyone over the phone.
- ☑ If you receive a call and the number is blocked do not give any personal information.

HAVE EVER HAD SOME CALL AND SAY YOU WON, AND THAN WANT YOUR CREDIT CARD NUMBER? AND WHAT DID YOU SAY OR DO?

Never give your credit card or check-ing account number to someone who calls you and tries to sell you some-thing or claims to need your account number to send you a "prize" or verify your account. Never give your credit card number, checking account number, or personal infor-mation to a caller.

TEEN/STUDENT APPROVED

Banking for Teens and Students- Book and Study Guide ---Adjusting Your Life Style by Bridget C. Williams